OVER THE HIMALAYA

KOICHIRO OHMORI

DIADEM BOOKS • LONDON

AN IMPRINT OF HODDER HEADLINE PLC

Copyright © 1994 by Koichiro Ohmori
Mountains of the Himalaya copyright © 1994 by Yugo Ono
First published in 1994 by Yama-Kei Publishers Co., Ltd.
English translation copyright © 1994 by Yama-Kei Publishers Co., Ltd.
Foreword copyright © 1994 by Chris Bonington

First published in Great Britain 1994 by Diadem Books.
Diadem Books is a division of Hodder Headline PLC
338 Euston Road, London NW1 3BH
British Library Cataloguing in Publication Data
A CIP catalogue record for this title is available from the British Library
ISBN 0 906371 15 5

Printed and bound in Singapore by Tien Wah Press

Contents

Foreword — Chris Bonington
Map of the Nepal Himalaya

	PLATES
Kangchenjunga region	1 — 6
Everest, Lhotse & Makalu	7 — 13
Khumbu Himal & the Rolwaling Himal	14 — 21
Langtang Himal, Jugal Himal & Ganesh Himal	22 — 27
Manaslu region	28 — 32
Annapurna Himal	33 — 39
Dhaulagiri region	40 — 44

Mountains of the Himalaya — Yugo Ono
Flying over the Himalaya — Koichiro Ohmori
About the photos — Yugo Ono

FOREWORD

I feel most honoured to have been asked to write the foreword to this book of magnificent photographs, ***Over the Himalaya,*** and am especially pleased to do so in view of the great tradition of mountaineering in Japan and the many fine achievements of Japanese climbers.

I have flown over the massive Himalayan peaks many times. Sometimes their towering ramparts are wreathed in cloud, but on a bright clear day every detail is visible. Even then, however, the views are fleeting; it is extremely difficult to capture them on film and only transitory images remain. This book allows those views to be savoured again and again. Not only that, it gives the opportunity to study the great peaks from a distance, prompts reflection on previous trips and inspires thoughts of future ventures. So many times when I was planning an expedition, especially to the impending South Face of Annapurna and the giant Southwest Face of Everest, and searching for every possible detail of the proposed routes, photographs of this quality, giving a panoramic view of the peak and its surrounding terrain, would have been invaluable.

Every time I return to the great Himalayan range, I never cease to be amazed by the majestic beauty, the sheer scale and vastness of the huge faces, soaring ridges and tortured ice-falls. I have experienced there some of the most inspiring moments of my life and also had my closest brushes with death.

Everest, of course, has played a major part in my mountaineering career and on reaching the summit myself at last in 1985, at the age of 50, having led three previous expeditions, I was overcome with a mixture of emotions. Thoughts flooded into my mind of all the friends I had lost over the years, not only on Everest itself but on other mountains, and I wept for them and also for the personal fulfilment I felt on finally reaching the highest point on earth.

I have so many wonderful memories of all my trips to the Himalaya spanning over thirty years — of the beauty and grandeur of the incomparable scenery, of the warmth and friendship of the local peoples, of many a struggle with hard technical climbing and the problems of altitude, often combined with a war of attrition with the weather. On my first visit to the range, which was in 1960 to attempt 7937m Annapurna II, there were no tourists or trekkers and very few expeditions. In Kathmandu there was only one hotel, very little traffic and the only road in Nepal was the one from the frontier at Raxaul to Kathmandu. We started our approach march in the outskirts of Kathmandu, walked around the west side of Annapurna, succeeded in making the first ascent and then walked out to its east, crossing the Tilicho Pass and descending the Kali Gandaki. In a period of three months we saw only two fellow foreigners — members of a Swiss expedition to Dhaulagiri. The foothills and the mountains had a pristine freshness, untouched by the presence of tourists.

The following year I went to Nuptse, the third peak of Everest. Sola Khumbu was as unspoiled as the Annapurna region. It was after climbing the South Face of Nuptse that I had my first glimpse of the Southwest Face of Everest, a massive wall of dark rock, veined in ice and snow. In 1961 I could not imagine anyone attempting it, let alone that I should lead the expedition that successfully climbed it.

From a distance the mountains of the Himalaya, as shown in this beautiful book, are as glorious as ever but I was particularly saddened when, on a visit to Nanga Parbat basecamp in 1990, I found it totally despoiled by the rubbish left by several mountaineering expeditions. Perhaps the greatest challenge facing every climber now, as on a global scale it faces mankind, is how we treat our mountain environment. There is a temptation to feel that an area as vast as the Himalayan chain is inviolable but it is becoming all too clear that this is not so. Many of the problems may seem beyond the climbers' control, such as over-population in the valleys leading to deforestation, and inappropriate development among the mountains themselves.

The essential motives and urge to climb remain as strong as they have always been; the feeling of wonder at the sheer beauty of ice, snow, rock and sky, the satisfaction of having faced and overcome risk, and an unquenchable curiosity to explore the unknown. But we have a responsibility to treat the mountains with respect and restraint, remove our own rubbish and encourage others to do the same, and climb in a way that does not leave permanent traces of our presence. With the explosion in the growth of expeditioning, trekking and tourism, bringing ever-increasing, often unsustainable, pressures to poorly resourced areas, pollution is becoming a problem. Therefore, one of the most important issues facing us today is the impact we make on the vulnerable mountain environment.

If climbers can successfully take up this challenge, they will be in a much stronger position to help influence the outcome of some of the wider issues affecting the future protection of the mountains so outstandingly illustrated in this book.

Chris Bonington
March 1994

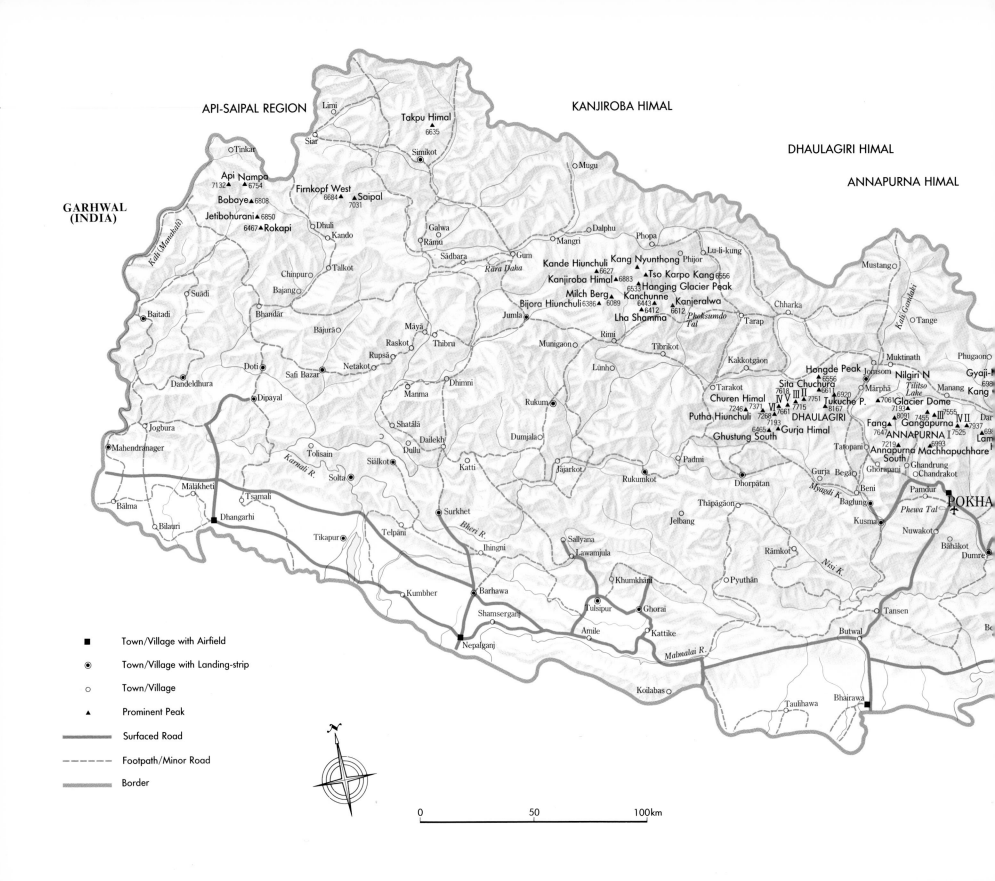

API-SAIPAL REGION

KANJIROBA HIMAL

DHAULAGIRI HIMAL

ANNAPURNA HIMAL

GARHWAL
(INDIA)

Town/Village with Airfield

Town/Village with Landing-strip

Town/Village

Prominent Peak

Surfaced Road

Footpath/Minor Road

Border

0   50   100km

NEPAL HIMALAYA

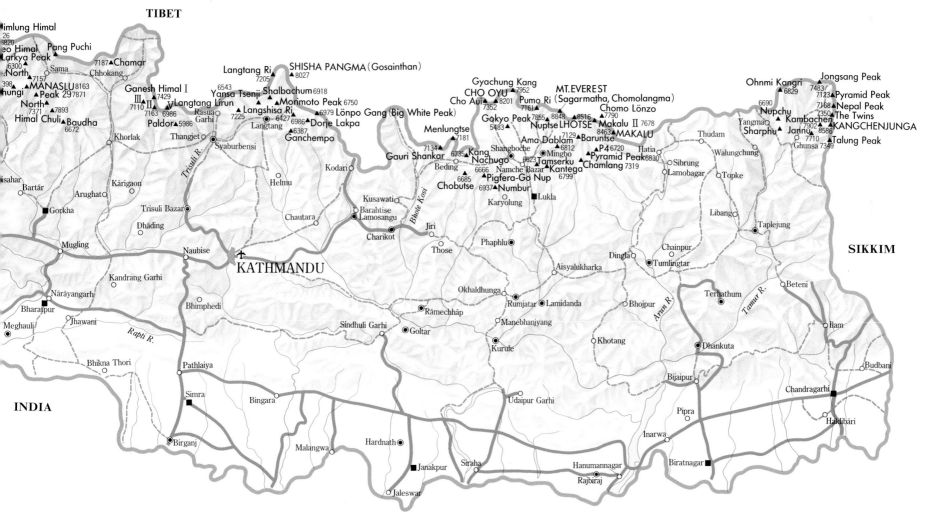

MANASLU REGION

LANGTANG HIMAL

EVEREST REGION

GANESH HIMAL

JUGAL HIMAL

KHUMBU HIMAL

KANGCHENJUNGA REGION

ROLWALING HIMAL

TIBET

imlung Himal
26
8820
eo Himal
Larkya Peak
6300
North
398
MANASLU 8163
hungi
Peak 29 7871
North
7371
7893
Himal Chuli
Baudha
6672

Pang Puchi

7187 ▲Chamar

Langtang Ri
7205

SHISHA PANGMA (Gosainthan)
▲ 8027

Gyachung Kang
CHO OYU 7952
Cho Aui 8201
7352
Pumo Ri
7161

MT.EVEREST
(Sagarmatha, Chomolangma)
Chomo Lönzo
7790

Ohnmi Kangri
6829

Jongsang Peak

7123▲Pyramid Peak

Nupchu
6690
7168▲Nepal Peak

Yangma
7350
The Twins
7483

Sama
7157
Chhokang

Ganesh Himal I
6543
Yansa Tsenji Shalbachum 6918
III 7429
7110 II Langtang Lirun
7163 6986 ▲Langshisa Ri
Rasua 6427 6986
Garhi 7225 6387
Paldor▲5986 Langtang
Thangjet Ganchempo

Morimoto Peak 6750
▲6979 Lönpo Gang (Big White Peak)
▲ Dorje Lakpa

Menlungtse
▲7181

Gokyo Peak 7855 8848
5483▲
Nuptse LHOTSE
Ama Dablam 8463 ▲Baruntse
▲6812 7129
Shangboche Mingbo P4 6720
6623▲Tamserku Pyramid Peak6830
Nachugo Namche Bazar Kantega 7319
6666 ▲ Chamlang
6799

Makalu II 7678
MAKALU

Kambachen
7902 8586
Sharphu▲ Jannu
7710
Ghunsa 7349 ▲Talung Peak

Khorlak

Kärigaon

Arughat

Gorkha

Khandrang Garhi

Trisuli Bazar

Dhading

Mugling

Naubise

Syaburbensi

Helmu

Kodari

Kusawati
Barahtise
Lamosangu

Charikot

Jiri

Those

Gauri Shankar
6735▲Kang
Beding
6685
Chobutse
6937▲Numbur

Karyolung

Lukla

Phaphlu

Aisyalukharka

Dingla

Chainpur
Tumlingtar

Thudam

Walungchung

Sibrung
Lamobagar

Topke

Libang

Taplejung

SIKKIM

Narayangarh

Bharatpur

Meghauli

Jhawani

Kandrang Garhi

Bhimphedi

Chautara

Rapti R.

KATHMANDU

Sindhuli Garhi

Goltar

Okhaldhunga

Rumjatar Lamidanda

Kurule

Bhojpur

Manebhanjyang

Khotang

Dhankuta

Terhathum

Tamur R.

Beteni

Ilam

Bhikna Thori

Pathlaiya

Simra

Bingara

Udaipur Garhi

Bijaipur

Pipra

Chandragarhi

INDIA

Birganj

Malangwa

Hardnath

Janakpur

Siraha

Hanumannagar

Inarwa

Biratnagar

Budbani

Haldibari

Jaleswar

Rajbiraj

KANGCHENJUNGA REGION

1. South Face of Jannu, 7710m, from the southwest
2. Jannu from the southwest
3. Jannu (right) and Kangchenjunga, 8586m, from the west
4. Kangchenjunga from the southwest, above the Yalung Glacier
5. Kangchenjunga from the northwest
6. Jongsang Peak, 7483m, from the south

3

4

6

Everest, Lhotse and Makalu

7. Everest, 8848m, and the Khumbu Glacier from the west-northwest

8. Everest and surrounding peaks from just south of Lhotse

9. Everest and surrounding peaks from the west

10. Southwest Face and the upper slopes of Everest from the west-northwest

11. East Face of Everest (left) and Makalu, 8463m, from the southeast

12. East Face of Everest (left) and Makalu from the south

13. Makalu from the southwest

8

KHUMBU HIMAL AND THE ROLWALING HIMAL

14. Ama Dablam, 6812m, from the northwest
15. Ama Dablam (right center) and the mountains of the Khumbu Himal from the northeast
16. Fluted face of an unnamed peak, 6340m, from east of Ama Dablam
17. Kantega, 6799m, (right) and Tamserku, 6623m, from the southeast
18. Gyachung Kang, 7952m, (right) and Cho Oyu, 8201m, from the southeast
19. Terminus of the Ngojumba Glacier and the Dudh Kosi viewed from upstream
20. Menlungtse, 7181m, from the south
21. Gauri Shankar from the south-southwest

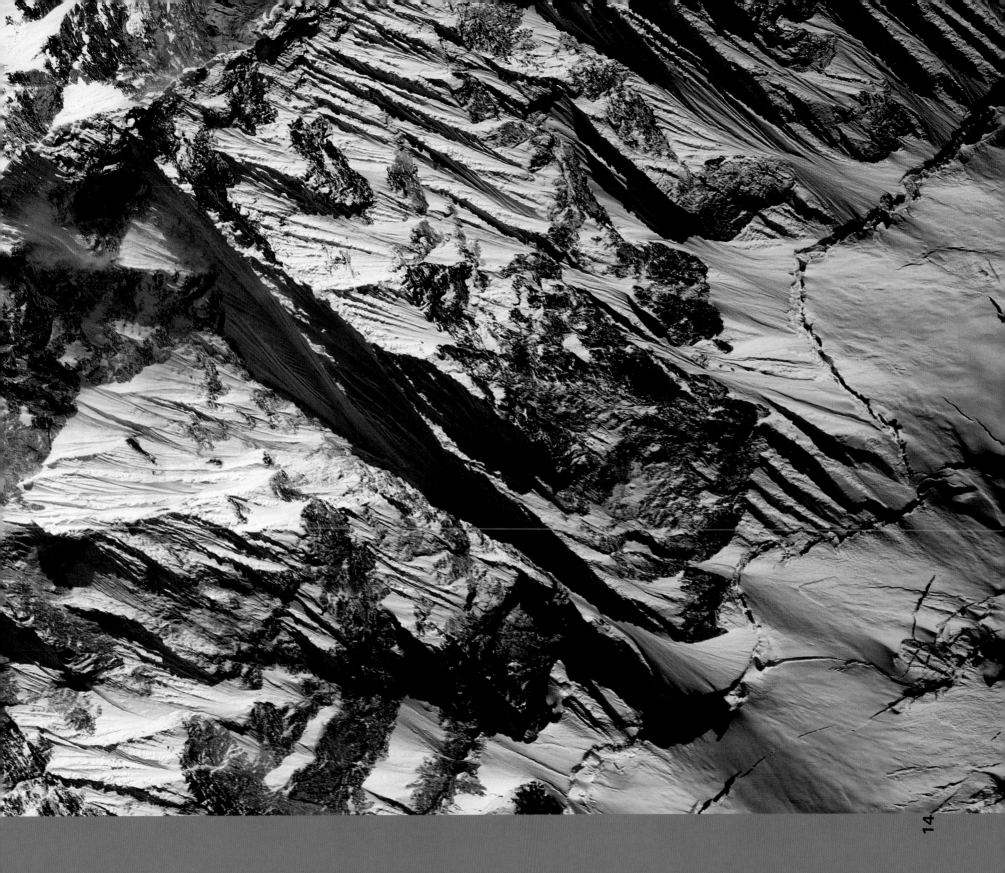

16

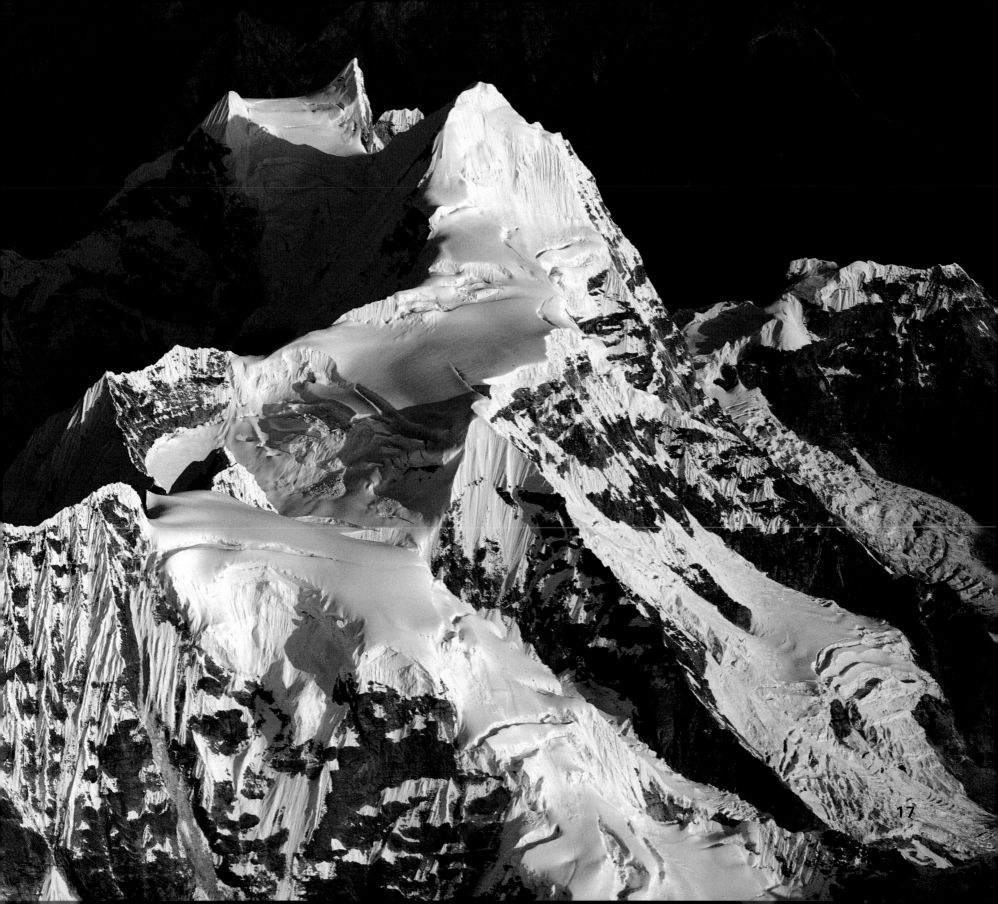

17

18

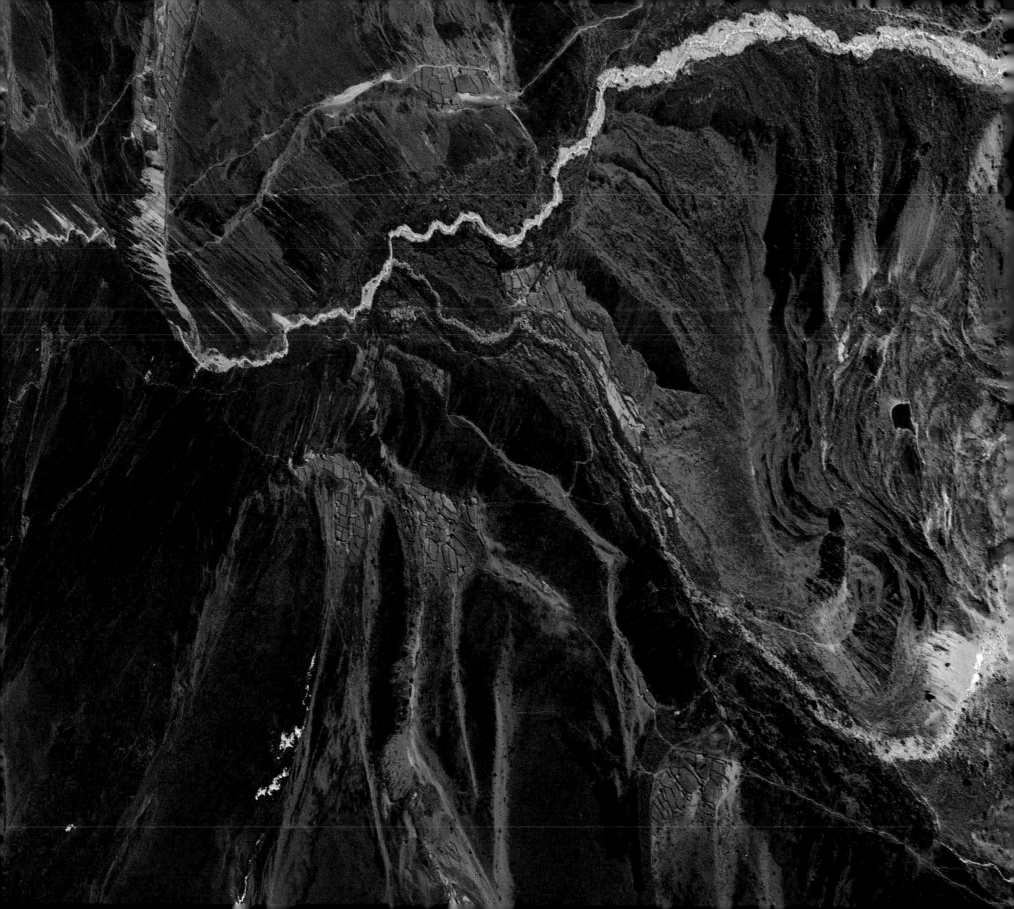

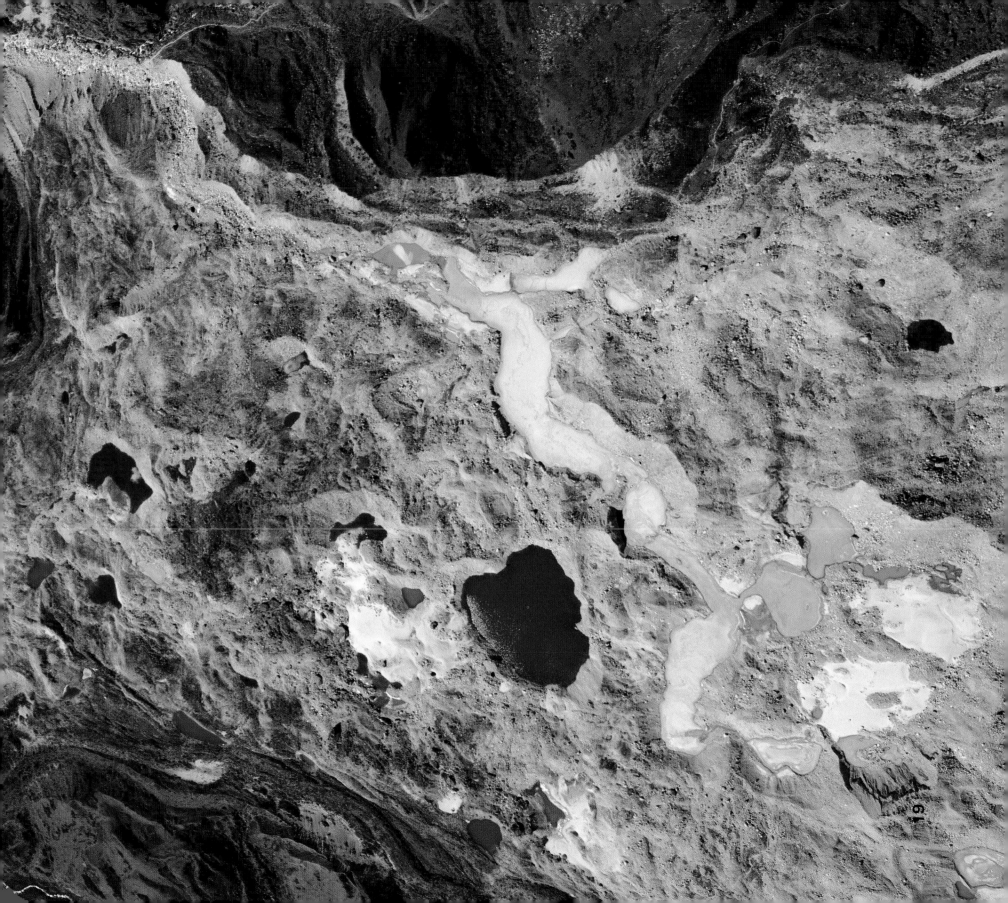

21

LANGTANG HIMAL, JUGAL HIMAL & GANESH HIMAL

22. Shisha Pangma, 8027m, from the southwest, above the Langtang Valley
23. Shisha Pangma and peaks surrounding the Langtang Valley from the southwest, above the Langtang Valley
24. Shisha Pangma and peaks of Langtang and Jugal Himal from the southwest
25. Mountains of Jugal, Rolwaling and Khumbu Himal from the northwest
26. Langtang Lirun, 7225m, (left) and peaks of the Langtang Himal from the southeast
27. Ganesh Himal, 7429m, from the south

MANASLU REGION

28. Manaslu, 8163m, from the southwest
29. Manaslu (left) and Himal Chuli, 7893m, from the northwest
30. Himal Chuli (right) and the Manaslu range from the south-southeast
31. Eastern side of Himal Chuli and the West Peak, 7540m, from the northeast
32. Himal Chuli from the north

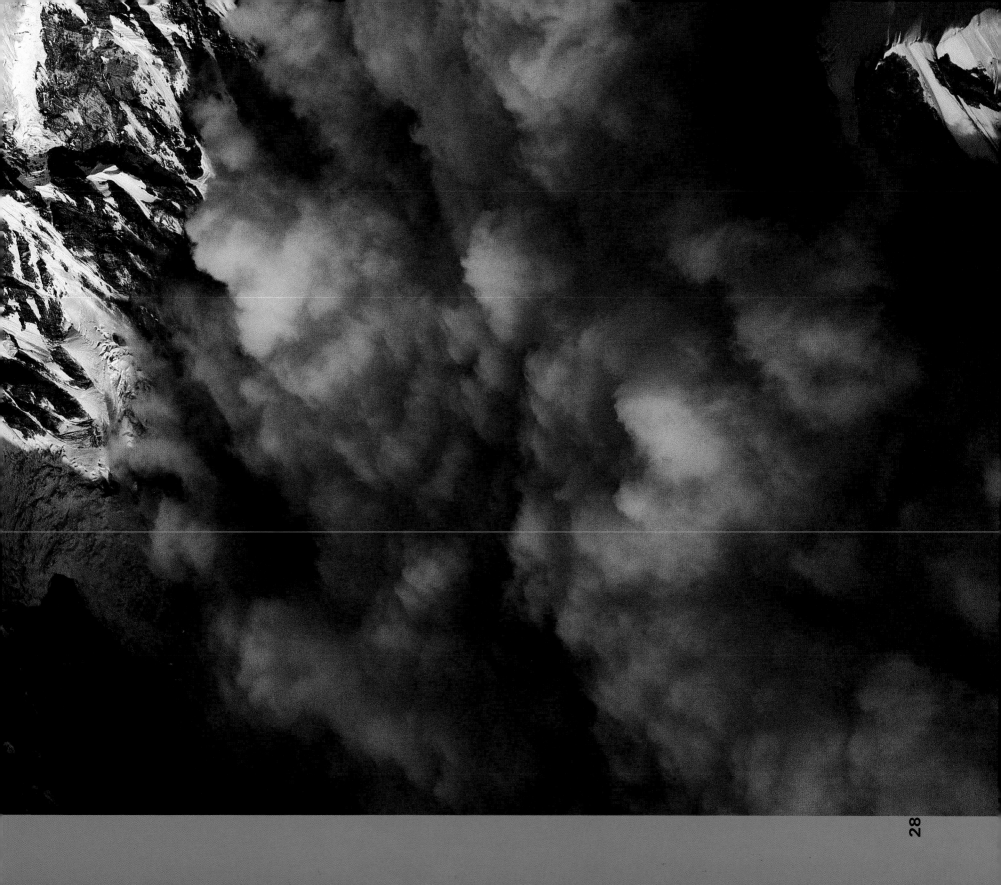

32

Annapurna Himal

33. Machhapuchhare, 6993m, from the north

34. Machhapuchhare (far right) and Gangapurna, 7455m, from the north

35. Annapurna I, 8091m, from the southeast

36. Overall view of the Annapurna Himal from the southeast

37. Annapurna II, 7937m, (right) and Lamjung Himal, 6983m, from the north

38. Annapurna I (far left) and Tilitso Himal, 7134m, (right) from the northeast

39. Annapurna Himal from the north-northwest, above Tilitso Lake

37

39

DHAULAGIRI REGION

40. South Face of Dhaulagiri I, 8167m, from the south

41. Dhaulagiri I from the east-southeast

42. Dhaulagiri I (left) and Dhaulagiri II, 7751m, from the east-northeast

43. Dhaulagiri I (upper left) and Tukuche Peak, 6920m, from the east-northeast

44. Putha Hiunchuli, 7246m, (upper left) and Churen Himal, 7371m, (right) from the east-southeast

45. The village of Phortse clings to a tiny bit of flat land

41

44

45

MOUNTAINS OF THE HIMALAYA
by Yugo Ono

FLYING OVER THE HIMALAYA
by Koichiro Ohmori

ABOUT THE PHOTOS
by Yugo Ono

MOUNTAINS OF THE HIMALAYA

by Yugo Ono

The Himalaya is the world's highest mountain range, bounded by the plains of India on the south and the Tibetan Plateau on the north. While the Ganges River delta is essentially at sea level, the average elevation of the Tibetan Plateau is 4500 meters, and it covers an area seven times as large as all of Japan. The Himalaya is a giant barrier of rock and ice, stretching east to west for 2400 km along the edge of the largest high plateau in the world.

At the western end of the Himalaya is the Indus River; the ninety-degree bend of the Brahmaputra River is the eastern border. Towering above this great bend is Namcha Barwa, the first ascent of which was recently completed by a joint Japanese-Chinese expedition. If the eastern end of Hokkaido were placed at this great bend, the Ryukyu Islands would lie along the Indus. It is as if the entire Japanese archipelago were raised by 4000 meters and placed along the southern edge of the Tibetan Plateau.

This analogy is not merely coincidental. Just as the Japanese archipelago was formed at the juncture of two great plates, the Eurasian and the Pacific, the Himalaya was formed at the juncture of the Eurasian Plate and the Indian Plate. Plate tectonics assumes that the earth's crust is made up of a number of plates which fit together like a giant jigsaw puzzle. Each plate is up to one hundred kilometers thick. This does not seem thin unless it's compared with the earth's radius of 6400 kilometers: a ratio comparable with that of the thickness of an egg shell and the whole egg.

All plates float atop a fluid mass called the asthenosphere, and they move several centimeters each year. India was attached to Africa 100,000,000 years ago; then it split apart and drifted northward until colliding with the Eurasian continent some 50,000,000 years ago.

This collision formed the Himalaya. Just as in a crash between a compact car and a large truck, the leading edge of the smaller Indian Plate was bent and subducted beneath the larger Eurasian Plate. The southern edge of the Eurasian Plate was lifted, forming the Himalaya. Before the plates collided, there was a broad sea between them. Multiple layers of sediment had been accumulating for several hundred million years on the bottom of this Tethys Sea. When the collision occured, the sea disappeared, and the material underlying the seabed was squeezed into a complicated structure.

The layers of sediment that had been flat while under the sea were both tilted and forced apart as they were lifted by the collision. It was this uplifting which produced the Himalaya. The most famous of these sedimentary layers is the Yellow Band that runs diagonally across the upper part of the southwest face of Mount Everest. Above this band of yellow-brown limestone, in a higher layer not far below Everest's summit, has been found a fossil sea lily of a type which lived on the shallow sea floor some half-billion years ago. This highly visible Yellow Band, some 8000 meters above sea level, is convincing proof that the entire Himalaya was once an ocean bottom.

BLACK MOUNTAINS AND WHITE MOUNTAINS

The Himalaya is made up of two types of mountains. The black mountains have summits formed by layers that were once part of the floor of the Tethys Sea. The white mountains are those from which the black upper layers have been stripped by erosion, exposing the plutonic rocks, such as granite that lie below. The lower half of the south-west face of Everest is whitish granite.

Most of the mountains whose summits were once part of the Tethys Sea's lower layers can be identified at a glance; the beautiful striped patterns formed by these layers run diagonally across the mountains' faces. This is particularly obvious in this book's photos of Gyachung in the Khumbu Himal. Putha Hiunchuli and Churen Himal in the Dhaulagiri Himal also clearly show that they are composed of sea bottom layers. As the Indian Plate approached from the south, the formerly flat layers were uplifted on their southern side and tilted toward the north, eventually running into the Tibetan Plateau.

When the Himalaya was uplifted, plutonic rocks such as granite were brought up from far below the earth's surface. Most of them changed their properties under the intense heat and pressure, becoming what is called metamorphic rocks. Some high peaks such as Kangchenjunga, Makalu and Manaslu are composed of this white rock all the way to their summits. Yet Everest, the highest, still has distinctive black sea-bottom layers which have been completely stripped from these mighty but lower peaks. There are still many secrets buried in these fascinating layers.

The panoramas in this volume cover the high peaks of the Nepal Himalaya, which occupies the central portion of the Great Himalaya. They are arranged from east to west.

THE KANGCHENJUNGA REGION

This region occupies the eastern end of the Nepal Himalaya, at the borders of India and Sikkim, and is centered on Kangchenjunga, the world's third highest mountain. The magnificent view of Kangchenjunga from Darjeerling, at the base of this range on the Sikkim side, has long been famous. Until the mid-19th century this was thought to be THE highest mountain.

This range consists of an east-west ridge along the Tibet-Nepal border and a north-south ridge along the Nepal-India border. The Tamur River bisects the two long ridges; it has four main tributaries which drain a large watershed. These two ridges intersect at Jongsang Peak, the point where Tibet, Nepal and India meet. The north-south ridge runs across Tent Peak and The Twins to Kangchenjunga, then continues southward to Talung Peak and Kabru. This long ridge is called the Singalila Range. The mysterious peak of Jannu forms a branch ridge to the Nepal side, while Siniolchu is the main peak on the Sikkim side.

THE KHUMBU HIMAL AND THE ROWALING HIMAL

Several major peaks, including Everest (called Chomolangma on the Tibetan side and Sagarmatha on the Nepal side), Lhotse and Makalu are in the Khumbu Himal. The Khumbu Himal is separated from the Kangchenjunga Himal by the deep gorge of the Arun River, which runs north-south through the Himalaya, and from the Rowaling Himal by the Dudh Kosi, which drains several major glaciers of the Khumbu Himal. The ridge along the Nepal-Tibet border runs west to east from Cho Oyu and Gyachung Kang across Pumo Ri to Everest, then across the South Col to Lhotse. From Lhotse a high ridge continues east to Makalu. To the south of these two highest ridges in the world is a north-south ridge joining several 7000-meter peaks including Ama Dablam, Kantega, Baruntse and Chamlang.

The Rowaling Himal, across the gorge of the Dudh Kosi, has only two summits above 7000 meters: Gauri Shankar and Menlungtse. It may be thought of as a frontal range leading up to the Khumbu Himal. To the west the Rowaling Himal is bounded by the gorge of the Bhote Kosi; before reaching the Langtang Himal, one must cross yet another deep gorge, that of the Sun Kosi.

THE LANGTANG HIMAL AND THE GANESH HIMAL

The Langtang Valley forms an eastern tributary of the valley of the Trisuli River, which flows from Tibet. It is a blind alley, ringed by 6000- and 7000-meter peaks, which compose the Langtang Himal. Shisha Pangma (Gosainthan) is slightly separated from the rest of the range, across the border in Tibet. The main ridge, which includes Langtang Lirun and Langtang Ri, runs along the Nepal-Tibet border. From Hagen's Col, which offers a closeup view of Shisha Pangma, this ridge runs southward to Lonpo Gang (Big White Peak), then southeasterly to Phurbi Chyachu. This ridge is also called the Jugal Himal. To the west, across the Trisuli River and between it and the gorge of the Burhi Gandaki, is the Ganesh Himal, running generally north-south.

THE MANASLU HIMAL

This range is separated from the Ganesh Himal by the gorge of the Burhi Gandaki, and from the Annapurna Himal by the gorge of the Marsyandi. It consists of a high north-south ridge along which are Manaslu, Peak 29, Ngadi Chuli and Himal Chuli. When one travels the road from Kathmandu to Pokhara, the three main peaks of the Manaslu Himal are visible on the right.

THE ANNAPURNA HIMAL

This long range runs from east to west, bounded on the east by the gorge of the Marsyandi and on the west by the gorge of the Kali Gandaki. The view of the Annapurna Himal from Pokhara, at the base of the range, is one of the most magnificant mountain vistas anywhere. The view of the high ridge, from Annapurna South (Annapurna Dakshin) across the sheer South Face of Annapurna I to Annapurna III and Annapurna II is overwhelming to most viewers. And, it that were not enough, the Matterhorn-like peak of Machhapuchhare towers in the foreground.

THE DHAULAGIRI HIMAL

This range is separated from the Annapurna Himal by the gorge of the Kali Gandaki, the deepest in the Himalaya. The main ridge runs north-south, parallel to the Kali Gandaki, from Tukuche Peak in the north to Dhaulagiri I in the south. Another ridge runs westward from Tukuche Peak across French Pass, then across Dhaulagiri I through V to Putha Hiunchuli. Dhaulagiri means "white mountain" in Sanskrit. The view from Pokhara of its white peak is most impressive. However, geologically it is one of the black mountains, with a striped pattern.

FLYING OVER THE HIMALAYA

by Koichiro Ohmori

It was pitch black, inside and out, when I awoke at three in the morning. Miss Machiko Tajika, manager of the Hotel Everest View, was already up. B. K. Shrestha, the mechanic, was grinning as he emerged from his room. I asked Machiko to wake Captain Duan, the pilot, then headed for the airstrip with the mechanic. After descending the trail by flashlight for thirty minutes the white silhouette of the airplane appeared through the trees at the end of the runway; it was a relief to see it.

As we removed the tie-down ropes, checked the aircraft, and wiped the morning dew from the windows the sky began to light up, and our flashlights were no longer necessary. Soon Michiko and the pilot arrived and he began his checks. The camera chest was secured to the seat while the flight map, computer, film, neutral density filter and air spray were arranged in their usual places, along with small but important items such as rubber bands and pencils.

Takeoffs in Nepal are permitted only after sunrise, though this particular runway was still in the shadow of Tamserku. Checking my watch, I told the pilot, "let's go." The down-sloping runway, pointed directly at Tamserku, quickly dropped beneath us as we headed south and gained altitude. Banking to the left, we climbed over the peaks of Khumbu. Beyond Baruntse, Everest and Makalu appeared in morning alpenglow. The snow plume streaming from Everest's summit alerted us to strong westery winds aloft. It was a magnificent morning.

I asked the pilot to climb higher and closer to the summits, but he declined and we turned slightly to the left. To climb higher would have placed us in the westerly wind while dropping lower would put us into a turbulent region. I thought how fortunate I was to have come to the Khumbu;

Kathmandu was almost certainly still fogged in, making take-offs there impossible. Staying in the thin layer of stable air, we gazed down on the glowing summits of the Khumbu.

After many years of climbing, I still believe the greatest satisfaction is the struggle to reach the summit by foot, particularly when the route is remote and difficult. Why, then, did I choose to photograph the "thrones of the gods" from the air?

In April 1960 I was in a tent at the Pokhara airstrip with the Keio University Alpine Club, waiting for our supplies to arrive. A Swiss expedition to Dhaulagiri was using a Pilatus Porter "Yeti" to ferry their supplies to 5200 meter Dhampus Pass north of Dhaulagiri. Having thought that mountains were only supposed to be climbed by foot, this first exposure to the use of aircraft in the mountains made a lasting impression. I could not then imagine that I would later find myself flying many times with one of those young pilots, Emil Wick, who, on that day, was making highballs with snow he'd brought down from Dhampus Pass.

Returning home from that expedition, I took out the rough charts we had used for reference. I had drawn these from aerial photographs taken for us by the Survey of India. With the photos I had taken during the expedition, together with several thousand photos borrowed from other expeditions, and with the assistance of the staff of Japan's Geographical Survey Institute, I produced a topograhic map of the Himal Chuli region; becoming deeply impressed with the value of aerial photographs in mountaineering.

When the Japanese Alpine Club was planning their attempt on the Southwest Face of Everest in 1970, I proposed reconnaissance using aerial photography. Tests were conducted in Japan, but my

proposed reconnaissance was called off at the last minute. It was particularly disappointing as I had hope that the survey would contribute to a successful climb. After the expedition was over, I proceeded on my own. As I expected, the survey went well. This deepened my confidence in the value of aerial photography for studying mountains, particularly the value of three-dimensional side views of very steep slopes.

For several years Himalayan climbing became far removed from my daily life as I was forced to immerse myself in the world of work. But I used my short vacations to visit Nepal, there to search for climbing routes from the air. Before I realized it, I became addicted to viewing the beauty of mountains as seen from above and to doing my best to capture that beauty on film.

It is exhilarating to see unscaled peaks and faces, to learn about an unknown world before anyone else. And then to have one's photos contribute to someone's successful climb. Although it lacks the satisfaction of putting one's own feet on a mountain, aerial photography offers a different type of gratification; perhaps that of the pioneers whose efforts motivate others.

As a fixed-wing airplane very quickly flys over any specific spot, there is a limit as to what one can see and remember with the naked eye, but a tremendous amount of information can be captured and stored in a photograph. Studying the details later, I often experience some of the thrill of an actual climb, if only vicariously.

To maximize the amount of information contained in a photo, I use a medium format (2¼") film and I have designed and made my own Aeromax 615 panorama cameras; this gives a 6x15cm negative or slide with roughly the same lateral field as two human eyes. Although Linhof and Fuji Film have since brought to the market panoramic cameras, I feel that mine still outperform the commercial models.

I had a great deal of assistance in making my cameras. The lenses were carefully selected, after testing numerous candidates, with the help of Yotaro Kobayashi of Fuji Xerox Co., Ltd. and Yasuo Honda of Fuji Photo Optical Co., Ltd.; the late Kentaro Hattori of Hattori Seiko Co., Ltd. helped with the special high-speed shutter; and a friend, Nobuji Iida, did the precision lathe machining. Although I have made eight cameras, most of my panoramas have been taken with the three having lenses with focal lengths of 90mm, 125mm and 150mm.

Aerial photography permits a much greater order of freedom than ground photography in choosing the angle from which a mountain is viewed. Conversely, flying technique becomes much more important than photographic technique. One has to consider the weather and the microscale winds created by the topography, then maneuver the plane to the desired location and altitude, at the desired time and at the desired angle. I am fortunate to have learned to fly light aircraft well enough to be able to do this. Even so, I still need an aircraft with the necessary capabilities, a skilled pilot, and oxygen. Not all of these are always available in Nepal. From 1971 to 1983 I made many flights with Captain Wick in a Pilatus Porter PC-6 equipped with a turbo engine. Occasionally we climbed to 9000 meters, where our oxygen supply system was inadequate. Due to an accident and mechanical difficulties the PC-6 became unavailable; I tried a Twin Otter several times but it could not climb well enough. For the next several years I had to be satisfied photographing the mountains of Switzerland and Japan.

Only later did I resolve to undertake a photographic survey of the entire range of the Nepal Himalaya when, at my instigation, Takashi Miyahara of Himalaya Kanko Kaihatsu ("Tourism Development") Co., Ltd., finally had the PC-6 repaired, and the plane became usable again in the Fall of 1990.

The Himalaya is both high and wide, thus the style of flying needed for aerial photography is quite different than elsewhere. In Europe and Japan one can usually anticipate conditions, then take off and fly by the selected subjects one by one. To approach the desired subject in the Himalaya, however, one must give detailed consideration to the weather, distance, time and light angles. Flight are limited to a maximum of three-and-a-half hours while altitudes are limited to not more than 1000 meters above the higher summits. Strong winds, low temperatures, and oxygen shortages can present serious problems for airplanes, cameras and people. All of these problems must be constantly controlled to achieve the desired objectives of every flight. But these challenges are what, for me, makes flying above the Himalaya so exciting.

There is virtually no reliable weather information available for the mountainous regions of Nepal. Even when a flight plan is made in advance, one must rely on every physical sensation, as well as instinct and experience, to have a reasonable chance of a successful and safe flight. Turbulence is always a major concern wherever high winds meet high mountains; even when there are no tell-tale clouds, one must always try to visualize where it might occur. Even though I like to think I know what to expect, I once flew directly into severe turbulence.

Flying over the Rowal Himal, I saw a beautiful face off to my right and maneuvered my plane to approach it downwind. Just as I loosened my seat belt to gain more freedom of movement, the plane was jolted by terrific turbulence. I pressed one hand against the ceiling for support while hanging onto my camera with the other. The view rapidly alternated between sky and valley. My light meter floated in front of my face. Several hundred pieces of candy that had been in a box were floating throughout the cabin. While I struggled desperately against the violent motions, the plane fell 3000 meters, emerging from the turbulence just above a glacier. We flew straight back to Syangboche, where Captain Shrestha and I laughed about how frightening it had been. He said, chuckling, "After, we can laugh!" Just another reminder from the gods of the Himalaya.

The list of problems I have encountered is lengthy. I have had to go without oxygen to conserve enough for the pilot. Controls have frozen at high altitude, causing the plane to fall rapidly. Rapid changes in air pressure have caused severe ear pain. I have been within a few minutes of approaching Everest only to have the engine misfire. The red warning light which indicates a clogged fuel filter has come on during the return flight, forcing me to watch the fuel guage closely to see if we could reach Kathmandu. One overnight snowfall made the mountains spectacularly beautiful, but by the time we removed all the snow from the aircraft there was no time left for the flight. Once, flying on the last day of my vacation, we landed in Kathmandu as my international flight was already on the runway; I had to quickly change clothes inside the small aircraft as we rushed to transfer my equipment to the larger plane.

Viewing mountains from the air seems to many as though it should always be easy and pleasant, but in real life it is almost always a series of problems. Thus the seriousness of the approach, overcoming the challenges, the excitement of reaching the objective and the feeling of accomplishment for me approach those of mountaineering itself.

The Himalaya has become almost a second home to me. Its mountains, like a mother in whose arms I hope to someday be cradled, tower above a world in which light and shadow are woven into majestic patterns. A glimpse of even a small part of that sublime world gives my heart a tremendous feeling of satisfaction. But there are still many peaks and faces that I have not yet seen, waiting for me. Will I ever see them all? And what new insights will I gain from them?

ABOUT THE PHOTOS

by Yugo Ono

EQUIPMENT

Camera: aeromax 615 (hand made) focal length∞
Lenses: Fujinon W150mm, 125mm
         Fujinon SW105mm
         Fujinon SW90mm
Shutter: an altered Seiko No. 0
Filters: skylight SL, 1B, ND2, centerfilter CF
Films: EPD, RDP, EH
Meter: Minolta spot meter M
Planes: Pilatus Porter PC-6
        Twin Otter
        Alouette III (helicopter)

Koichiro Ohmori, M. J. Shrestha (pilot) and the Pilatus Porter PC-6

> NOTE: Elevations of mountains are based on a list published by the government of Nepal in 1983, but the spelling of mountain names do not always agree.

1. SOUTH FACE OF JANNU FROM THE SOUTHWEST
① **Jannu, 7710m** ② **Jonsang Peak, 7483m**
③ **Yalung Kang (Kangchenjunga West Peak), 8505m**
④ **Kangchenjunga, 8586m** ⑤ **Yamatari Glacier**
⑥ **Jannu South Ridge**

    Jannu was first climbed on 27 April 1962 by a French team led by Lionel Terray. Their route led from the Yamatari Glacier up a tributary glacier, then from the shelf-like upper end of the glacier in the photo up the South Ridge at the right. The second ascent, by a Japanese team in 1974, followed the same route.

2. JANNU FROM THE SOUTHWEST
① **Jannu, 7710m** ② **Jannu South Ridge**
③ **Jannu Southwest Ridge** ④ **Jannu East Face**
⑤ **a Yalung Glacier tributary**

    In 1978 a British team led by Rab Carrington attempted to climb the East Face from the tributary of the Yalung Glacier, but turned back at 6500m. Switching to the Yamatari Glacier, and without oxygen, tents or Sherpas, they did the fourth ascent via the French Route in only five days. The first ascent of the Southwest Ridge was done by a Czech team led by A. Brazej in 1981.

3. JANNU AND KANGCHENJUNGA FROM THE WEST
① **Jannu, 7710m** ② **Jannu North Face**
③ **Jannu Southwest Ridge** ④ **Jannu East Ridge**
⑤ **Kambachen, 7902m**
⑥ **Yalung Kang (Kangchenjunga West Peak), 8505m**
⑦ **Kangchenjunga, 8586m** ⑧ **Kangchenjunga Central Peak, 8482m**
⑨ **Kangchenjunga South Peak, 8476m**

    The difficult North Face was first climbed in 1976 by a Japanese team led by Masatsugu Konishi. It was the third ascent of Jannu.

4. KANGCHENJUNGA FROM THE SOUTHWEST, ABOVE THE YALUNG GLACIER

① **Kambachen, 7902m**
② **Yalung Kang (Kangchenjunga West Peak), 8505m**
③ **Main Peak, 8586m** ④ **Central Peak, 8482m**
⑤ **South Peak, 8476m**
⑥ **the plateau below the summit, known as the "Great Shelf"**

The main peak of Kangchenjunga was first climbed in 1955 by a British team led by Charles Evans. The West Peak was first climbed in 1973 by a Japanese team, via the Southwest Face.

5. KANGCHENJUNGA FROM THE NORTHWEST

① **The Twins, 7350m** ② **Kangchenjunga, 8586m**
③ **Yalung Kang (Kangchenjunga West Peak), 8505m**
④ **Kambachen, 7902m** ⑤ **White Wave, 6960m**
⑥ **Kangchenjunga North Face** ⑦ **headwall of the Jannu Glacier**

The first attempt on the North Face route was in 1930, by an international expedition led by G. O. Dyhrenfurth. They were turned back by avalanches. Doug Scott, Peter Boardman and Joe Tasker made the first ascent of the North Ridge in 1979.

The North Face was first climbed in 1980 by a Japanese team.

6. JONGSANG PEAK FROM THE SOUTH

① **Jongsang Peak, 7483m** ② **outlier, 7090m** ③ **Lashar II, 6860m**

The main peak of Jongsang Peak is at the point where the international borders of China, Nepal and India converge. With a major cirque immediately beneath the summit, the mountain presents quite a unique sight, being almost completely covered by glaciers.

The first ascent was in 1930 by the international expedition led by G. O. Dyhrenfurth that had first attempted Kangchenjunga. They crossed the Jongsang La, circled to the northwest side, and completed the first ascent.

7. EVEREST AND THE KHUMBU GLACIER FROM THE WEST-NORTHWEST

① **Everest (Sagarmatha, Chomolangma), 8848m**
② **Lhotse, 8516m** ③ **Makalu, 8463m** ④ **Kangchenjunga, 8586m**
⑤ **the Western Cwm** ⑥ **the Khumbu Icefall**

The 1953 first ascent route of the British team led by John Hunt led directly up the Khumbu Icefall, through the Western Cwm, then via the South Col and the Southeast Ridge to the summit.

Extending from the left down into the foreground is the West Ridge, first climbed in 1963 by Americans Tom Hornbein and Willie Unsoeld, who also did the first Himalayan traverse when they descended via the South Col.

8. EVEREST AND SURROUNDING PEAKS FROM JUST SOUTH OF LHOTSE

① **Everest, 8848m** ② **Everest Southwest Face**
③ **Everest West Ridge** ④ **Everest Southeast Ridge**
⑤ **Lhotse, 8516m** ⑥ **Lhotse Shar, 8400m** ⑦ **Nuptse, 7855m**
⑧ **Pumo Ri, 7161m** ⑨ **Kala Patar, 5545m**
⑩ **the Khumbu Glacier** ⑪ **the Nuptse Glacier**

A frontal view of the great Lhotse-Nuptse barrier on the southern side of Mount Everest. An ascent of the South Face of Lhotse was claimed by Tomo Cesen of Slovenia in 1990.

9. EVEREST AND SURROUNDING PEAKS FROM THE WEST

① **Everest, 8848m** ② **Lhotse, 8516m** ③ **Nuptse, 7855m**
④ **Chomo Lönzo, 7790m** ⑤ **Kangchungtse (Makalu II), 7678m**
⑥ **Makalu, 8463m** ⑦ **Changtse, 7553m**

The towering peak just south of Everest across the South Col is Lho(south)tse(peak). The summit of the long ridge extending west from Lhotse is Nup(west)tse. Lhotse was first climbed by a Swiss team in 1956, Nuptse by a British team in 1961.

10. SOUTHWEST FACE AND UPPER EVEREST FROM THE WEST-NORTHWEST

① **Everest, 8848m** ② **Everest Southwest Face**
③ **Everest West Ridge** ④ **Everest Southeast Ridge**
⑤ **the Yellow Band** (a layer of Paleozoic limestone)
⑥ **Everest Northeast Ridge**

The Northeast Ridge was attempted by seven British expeditions, from 1921 through 1938. It was finally completed by a Chinese team in 1960. Peter Boardman and Joe Tasker disappeared high on the Northeast Ridge in 1982. In 1975 a British team led by Chris Boning

11. EAST FACE OF EVEREST AND MAKALU FROM THE SOUTHEAST

① **Everest, 8848m** ② **Lhotse, 8516m**
③ **Everest East Face (Kangshung Face)** ④ **Makalu, 8463m**
⑤ **Chomo Lönzo, 7790m** ⑥ **Makalu Southeast Ridge**
⑦ **Makalu Northeast Ridge**

The eastern side of Makalu contains a giant cirque, between the Southeast and Northeast Ridges. The glacial scouring which formed this cirque is more apparent in this photo than in the view from the west (photo 13). The East (Kangshung) Face of Everest was first climbed in 1983 by an American team.

12. EAST FACE OF EVEREST AND MAKALU FROM THE SOUTH

① **Cho Oyu, 8201m** ② **Gyachung Kang, 7952m**
③ **Nuptse, 7855m** ④ **Chamlang, 7319m** ⑤ **Everest, 8848m**
⑥ **Lhotse, 8516m** ⑦ **Baruntse, 7129m** ⑧ **Kamalu, 8463m**

The long ridges of Chamlang ("Great Flapping Bird" in Tibetan) cradle the source of the Iswa Glacier. A Japanese team led by Seiki Nakano made the first ascent in 1962, via the South Ridge, the long ridge extending into the left foreground.

13. MAKALU FROM THE SOUTHWEST

① Makalu, 8463m ② Chago Glacier ③ Sherpani Col
④ Lower Barun Glacier ⑤ Makalu Northwest Ridge
⑥ Makalu West Ridge ⑦ Makalu Southeast Ridge
⑧ Makalu South Face

Makalu was first climbed in 1955, via the Northwest Ridge, by a French team led by Jean Franco. The second ascent was by a Japanese team in 1970, via the Southeast Ridge. The West Ridge was first climbed in 1971 by a French team. The South Face was first climbed in 1975 by a Yugoslav team.

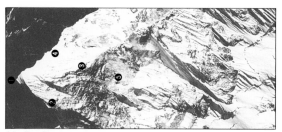

14. AMA DABLAM FROM THE NORTHWEST

① Ama Dablam, 6812m ② Ama Dablam North Ridge
③ Ama Dablam Northwest Ridge ④ Ama Dablam Southwest Ridge
⑤ Ama Dablam Northwest Face

This steep-sided peak towers above the "Everest Highway" at the entrance to the Khumbu Glacier. In the Sherpa language, ama means *"mother"* and dablam means *"neck ornament."* Ama Dablam was first climbed in 1961 by a New Zealand expedition led by Edmund Hillary. The North (Northeast) Ridge was first climbed in 1979 by a French team, while the Northwest Ridge was first climbed in 1980 by a Japanese expedition.

15. AMA DABLAM AND THE KHUMBU HIMAL FROM THE NORTHEAST

① Mera Peak, 6473m ② Kusum Kanguru, 6367m
③ Kantega, 6799m ④ Tamserku, 6623m ⑤ Karyolung, 6511m
⑥ Numbur, 6937m ⑦ Ama Dablam, 6812m
⑧ Hunku Nup Glacier

In this view from the heart of the Khumbu Himal, Ama Dablam towers over the south side of the Imja Glacier; behind it are Kantega and Tamserku. The deep gorge of the Dudh Kosi lies beneath the clouds. In the background are peaks of the Rolwaling Himal, including Numbur and Karyolung.

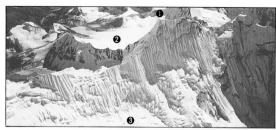

16. FLUTED FACE OF AN UNNAMED PEAK, FROM EAST OF AMA DABLAM

① unnamed peak, 6340m ② Hunku Nup Glacier
③ Chhukhung Glacier

The ice walls surrounding the great Himalayan peaks have countless grooves that appear to have been carved out with a knife. This is called "fluting." Just how such beautiful and regular patterns are formed is not yet fully understood. Factors which likely affect their development include avalanches, strong winds, low temperatures and sublimation of snow when strong sunlight strikes a dry snow surface. The right combination of conditions seems to occur frequently in the Himalaya, the "throne of the gods."

17. KANTEGA AND TAMSERKU FROM THE SOUTHEAST

① Tamserku, 6623m ② Kantega, 6799m ③ Khumjung village

A glacier forms when snow accumulates without melting and, under pressure, turns into ice, then begins to flow. In the precipitous Himalaya, glaciers cannot form where the terrain is too steep for snow to accumulate.

Kantega was first climbed in 1963 by a New Zealand expedition led by Edmund Hillary. In Tibetan kang means a *"snowy mountain"* and taiga a *"saddle."* Tamserku was also first climbed by another New Zealand team led by Hillary, in 1964.

18. GYACHUNG KANG AND CHO OYU FROM THE SOUTHEAST

① Nangpai Gosum (the long ridge on the south side of Cho Oyu)
② Cho Oyu, 8201m ③Gyachung Kang, 7952m ④Nup La, 5985m
⑤ West Rongbuk Glacier ⑥ Ngojumba Kang I, 7743m
⑦ Ngojumba Kang II, 7646m ⑧ Ngojumba Glacier

Cho Oyu, which means *"turquoise god"* in Tibetan, was first climbed by a three-man Austrian team led by Herbert Tichy in 1954. Gyachung Kang was first climbed in 1964, from the Ngojumba Glacier, by a Japanese team led by K. Kohara.

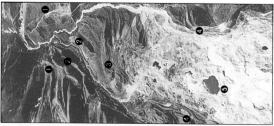

19. TERMINUS OF THE NGOJUMBA GLACIER AND THE DUDH KOSI

① a moraine formed when the glacier was advancing, above it is a kharka *(summer pasture)* ② a newer moraine
③ a "rock glacier" formed by folding of rocks on the ice glacier
④ the newest moraine ⑤ a frozen pond

When a glacier advances, it pushes rocks ahead of it, just like a bulldozer. These rocks are deposited in long banks, called *moraines*. Rocks falling from surrounding cliffs also come to rest on the glacier, frequently producing a very uneven surface.

20. MENLUNGTSE FROM THE SOUTH

① Menlungtse Main Peak, 7181m ② Menlungtse West Peak, 7023m

Menlungtse is the highest peak of the Rolwaling Himal. The West Peak was first climbed in 1988 via the West Face by a British team led by Chris Bonington. The Main Peak was first climbed in the fall of 1992 via the Southwest Face by A. Stremfelj and M. Prezelj of Slovenia.

Viewed from the south, the summit appears flat, with the Main Peak and the West Peak forming small rises at both ends. This photograph shows a rare bird's-eye view from above the mountain to the south, showing the glacier in the saddle between the two peaks

21. GAURI SHANKAR FROM THE SOUTH-SOUTHWEST

① Gauri Shankar Main Peak, 7134m
② Gauri Shankar South Peak, 7010m

Gauri Shankar is one of the best-known peaks in the Rowaling Himal. Viewed from Kathmandu, it is in a direct line with Everest, thus having been frequently overlooked. It was first climbed in 1979 by an American-Nepalese group led by Al Read, via the West Face (behind the ridge at the left). The South Peak was first climbed later that same year by a British team led by Peter Boardman.

In the local dialect it is pronounced "Gori Shankar," which means *"shining lucky omen."*

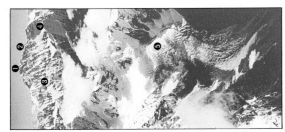

22. SHISHA PANGMA FROM THE SOUTHWEST, ABOVE LANGTANG VALLEY

① **Shisha Pangma, 8027m** ② **Phola Gangchen, 7661m**
③ **Goldum (Gosainthan), 6447m** ④ **Penthang Ri, 6842m**
⑤ **Sharbachum Glacier**

Shisha Pangma, the lowest of the fourteen 8000-meter peaks, was also the last to be climbed, by a Chinese expedition led by Hsu Ching in 1964. On the Nepal-India side it is called Gosainthan (Gosain = *holy*, than = *place*), and it has long been known by this name. It is immediately behind the Langtang Valley on the Nepal side, but is hidden by the mountains along the Tibetan border. One must climb from the valley to a high col to view it.

23. SHISHA PANGMA AND THE LANGTANG VALLEY FROM THE SOUTHWEST

① **Shisha Pangma, 8027m**
② **Penthang Karpo Ri (Dome Blanc), 6830m**
③ **Penthang Ri, 6842m** ④ **Goldum, 6447m**
⑤ **Triangle, 6800m** ⑥ **Langtang Glacier**

In 1949 the British explorer H. W. Tilman was the first to probe the Langtang Valley, which he described as "the most beautiful valley anywhere." At that time it was not clear whether Shisha Pangma was in Tibet. Penthang Karpo Ri was first climbed in 1955 by a Swiss team led by Raymond Lambert.

24. SHISHA PANGMA, THE LANGTANG AND JUGAL HIMAL FROM THE SW

① **Risum, 7133m** ② **Penthang Karpo Ri, 6830m**
③ **Shisha Pangma, 8027m** ④ **Phola Gangchen, 7661m**
⑤ **Nyanang Ri, 7071m** ⑥ **Dorje Lakpa, 6986m**
⑦ **Lönpo Gang (Big White Peak), 7083m** ⑧ **Gyalzen Peak, 6151m**

The mountains that extend eastward from the Langtang Valley form the Jugal Himal. The highest peak of this range, Lönpo Gang, was first climbed in 1962 by a Japanese expedition led by Akira Takahashi.

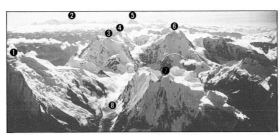

25. PEAKS OF JUGAL, ROLWALING AND KHUMBU HIMAL FROM THE NW

① **Penthang Karpo Ri, 6830m** ② **Everest, 8848m**
③ **Gur Karpo Ri, 6847m** ④ **Lönpo Gang, 7083m**
⑤ **Gauri Shankar, 7134m** ⑥ **Dorje Lakpa, 6986m**
⑦ **Langshisa Ri, 6427m** ⑧ **Langshisa Glacier**

Dorje Lakpa is the second highest peak of the Jugal Himal, after Lönpo Gang. This sharp peak, which is visible from Kathmandu, was first climbed in 1981 by a joint Japanese-Nepalese expedition led by K. Kataoka.

26. LANGTANG LIRUN AND THE LANGTANG HIMAL FROM THE SOUTHEAST

① **Naya Kanga, 5844m** ② **Ghenge Liru (Langtang II), 6571m**
③ **Langtang Lirun, 7225m** ④ **Kanja La, 5122m**
⑤ **Kimshun, 6745m** ⑥ **Yansa Tsenji, 6543m**
⑦ **Ponggen Dopku, 5930m**

Langtang Lirun is the highest peak of the Langtang Himal. First attempted in 1959 by a Japanese team led by Tetsuo Yamada, it was finally climbed by another Japanese expedition, led by Akira Ban, in 1978.

27. GANESH HIMAL FROM THE SOUTH

① **Ganesh Himal IV (Pabir), 7052m**
② **Ganesh Himal II (Lapsang Karbo), 7163m**
③ **Ganesh Himal I (Yangra), 7429m** ④ **Ganesh Himal V, 6986m**

Ganesh Himal IV, named after the Hindu deity Pabir *(elephant)*, does indeed resemble an elephant with its trunk hanging down to the right. The name Ganesh itself comes from the Hindu deity Ganesha, who has the head of an elephant. Ganesh Himal I was first climbed in 1955, by a Swiss-French expedition led by Raymond Lambert.

28. MANASLU FROM THE SOUTHWEST

① **Manaslu, 8163m** ② **Manaslu Southwest Ridge**
③ **Thulagi Glacier** ④ **Peak 29 Northwest Ridge**

After two failures, Manaslu was first climbed in 1955 by the third Japanese Alpine Club expedition, led by Aritune Maki. Their first ascent route was up the Northeast Face. The Southwest Face, seen in this photograph, was attempted by an Austrian expedition led by W. Nairz in 1972. One team member, Reinhold Messner, climbed solo to the summit in spite of losing his way on the plateau which can be seen in Photograph 29.

29. MANASLU AND HIMAL CHULI FROM THE NORTHWEST

① **Manaslu, 8163m** ② **Pinnacle, 7895m**
③ **Manaslu North Peak, 7157m** ④ **North Col**
⑤ **Manaslu West Ridge** ⑥ **Himal Chuli, 7893m**
⑦ **Himal Chuli West Peak, 7540m**
⑧ **Himal Chuli North Peak, 7371m**

The third Japanese Alpine Club expedition in 1956 set up their last camp on the large plateau on the north side of Manaslu. It was also here that two members of the 1972 Austrian expedition, which first climbed the Southwest Face, perished when they were unable to find their tent in a blizzard.

30. HIMAL CHULI AND THE MANASLU RANGE FROM THE SOUTH-SOUTHEAST

① **Manaslu, 8163m** ② **Peak 29 (Ngadi Chuli), 7871m**
③ **Himal Chuli North Peak, 7371m**
④ **Himal Chuli West Peak, 7540m** ⑤ **Himal Chuli, 7893m**

Himal Chuli was first climbed in 1960, from the west, by a Japanese group. The second ascent, in 1978, by another Japanese team, did the first ascent of the Southwest Face from the Dordi Khola. They also climbed the West Peak. Peak 29 was first climbed in 1970 by two members of a Japanese team but, unfortunately, both of them perished on the descent.

31. The eastern side and West Peak of Himal Chuli, from the NE
① Himal Chuli Main Peak, 7893m ② Himal Chuli West Peak, 7540m

Himal Chuli means *"sharp snow peak"* in Nepali. True to its name, it presents a varied topography, with gradual glacier-covered slopes interspersed with sharp rocky peaks. As seen in Photo 30, there is a gently sloping saddle between the Main Peak and the West Peak; this saddle was the route of the first ascent. The first ascent was by a Keio University team of which the author was a member. In support of the summit assault, he spent four days on a snow slope on the far side of the snowy ridge that extends to the right from the West Peak in this photograph.

32. Himal Chuli from the north
① Baudha Peak, 6672m ② Himal Chuli Main Peak, 7893m
③ Himal Chuli West Peak, 7540m
④ Himal Chuli North Peak, 7371m

The East Ridge of Himal Chuli is seen here as a long ridge extending into the left foreground. A 1958 Japanese Alpine Club reconnaissance expedition climbed this ridge to 6400m; in 1959 their main expedition reached 7400m, just below the main ridge, before retreating. A 1977 Meiji University team finally reached the main ridge but turned back just short of the summit.

Baudha Peak was first climbed in 1970 by a Keio University team.

33. Machhapuchhare from the north
① Machhapuchhare, 6993m ② Seti Khola

Machhapuchhare means *"fish's tail"* in Nepali. When Machhapuchhare is viewed from the north, there are, as suggested by the name, two peaks at the tip of a long ridge extending from Annapurna III. However, when viewed from Pokhara, the two peaks are superimposed and appear as one, giving this mountain the nickname "Matterhorn of the Himalaya." To the left is the deep gorge of the Seti Khola. In the background are 2000m peaks in central and southern Nepal.

34. Machhapuchhare and Gangapurna from the north
① Annapurna III, 7555m ② Machhapuchhare, 6993m
③ Gangapurna, 7455m

Annapurna III was first climbed in 1961 by an Indian expedition led by M. S. Kohli. The second ascent was by a Japanese Women's Climbing Club team led by Eiko Miyazaki, in 1970, from the East Annapurna Glacier via the col between Annapurna III and Gangapurna, seen here in the foreground.

In 1957 two members of a British team led by Jimmy Roberts climbed to 50m below the summit of Machhapuchhare, then retreated to keep a promise not to set foot on the summit, as this is a holy mountain.

35. Annapurna I South Face from the southeast
① Annapurna South (Annapurna Dakshin) 7219m
② Fang (Varaha Shikar), 7647m
③ Annapurna I, 8091m ④ Annapurna South Face

Annapurna I was first climbed in 1950 by a French team led by Maurice Herzog; the first ascent of an 8000m peak. In 1970 a British team led by Chris Bonington did the 4000m high South Face, the first big Himalayan face to be climbed. In 1981 a Polish team climbed the right-hand ridge to the Central Peak and a Japanese team did a new route in the center of the face.

36. An overall view of the Annapurna Himal from the southeast
① Annapurna South (Annapurna Dakshin), 7219m
② Fang (Varaha Shikar), 7647m ③ Annapurna I, 8091m
④ Dhaulagiri I, 8167m ⑤ Machhapuchhare, 6993m
⑥ Annapurna III, 7555m, ⑦ Annapurna IV, 7525m
⑧ Annapurna II, 7937m ⑨ Lamjung Himal, 6983m
⑩ Modi Khola Valley ⑪ Seti Khola Valley

Monsoon clouds approaching from the Indian Ocean are blocked by the Annapurna Himal. This is why the mountains on the Tibetan side, in the background in this photo, are so dry.

37. Annapurna II and Lamjung Himal from the North
① Lamjung Himal, 6983m ② Annapurna II, 7937m

The slopes near the summit of Annapurna II are too steep for glaciers, so that exposed rock faces dominate. In contrast, Lamjung Himal, with its more gradual slopes, is completely covered by glaciers.

Annapurna II was first climbed in 1960 by a British-Indian-Nepalese team led by Jimmy Roberts. The North Ridge, in the foreground, and the North Face are still unclimbed. Lamjung Himal was first climbed in 1974 by a British team led by Michael Burgess, via the East Ridge.

38. Annapurna I and Tilitso Himal from the northeast
① Roc Noir (Kangsar Kang), 7485m ② Annapurna I East Peak
③ Annapurna I, 8091m ④ Tilitso Himal, 7134m
⑤ Nigiri North, 7061m

Herzog's 1950 French team that did the first ascent of Annapurna I wandered around the base of the mountain for some time because of map errors. The "Grand Barrier," as they called the long ridge in the middle of this photograph, was not on their map; so their planned frontal assault was diverted via the Miristi Khola. This delay led to an epic retreat after the summit was reached.

39. Annapurna Himal from the North-northwest, above Tilitso Lake
① Annapurna II, 7937m ② Annapurna IV, 7525m
③ Annapurna III, 7555m ④ Gangapurna, 7455m
⑤ Machhapuchhare, 6993m ⑥ Roc Noir (Kangsar Kang), 7485m
⑦ Annapurna I, 8091m ⑧ Tilitso Lake

The topography of the northern side of Annapurna can be clearly seen here. Had this photograph been available in 1950, perhaps the French expedition would not have wasted weeks. A "Grand Barrier" confronted the expedition, which had planned to reach the base of Annapurna I directly from Tilitso Lake.

40. The South Face of Dhaulagiri I from the South
① Dhaulagiri I, 8167m ② Dhaulagiri I South Ridge
③ Dhaulagiri I South Face ④ Dhaulagiri I Southeast Ridge

From the bottom of the deep gorge of the Kali Gandaki, which runs north-south through the Himalaya, Dhaulagiri I rises straight up for 6000 meters. The South Face is one of the steepest and most difficult faces anywhere.

In 1977 Reinhold Messner led an international team on an attempt of the South Face, but they were forced back by powerful avalanches. A Japanese team made the first ascent of the Southeast Ridge, but lost four members.

41. Dhaulagiri I from the East-Southeast
① Dhaulagiri I, 8167m ② Dhaulagiri I South Ridge
③ Dhaulagiri I Southeast Ridge ④ Dhaulagiri I Northeast Ridge
⑤ Dhaulagiri I South Face ⑥ Dhaulagiri I East Face
⑦ Churen Himal, 7371m ⑧ Dhaulagiri IV, 7661m
⑨ Dhaulagiri II, 7751m

Dhaulagiri I was the initial objective of Maurice Herzog's French team, which made the first ascent of Annapurna in 1950. They looked for routes on the eastern and northern sides, but thought them impossible. The first ascent was in 1960 by a Swiss team led by Max Eiselin, via the Northeast Ridge.

42. Dhaulagiri I and Dhaulagiri II from the East-Northeast
① Dhaulagiri I, 8167m ② Dhaulagiri I North Face
③ Dhaulagiri I Northwest Ridge ④ Dhaulagiri II, 7751m
⑤ Dhaulagiri III, 7715m ⑥ Dhaulagiri V, 7618m

Dhaulagiri II, here seen towering across the gorge of the Myagdi Khola, was first climbed in 1971 by an Austrian team led by Franz Huber.

In 1979 a Japanese team led by Michiko Takahashi completed a traverse of Dhaulagiri II, III and IV.

43. Dhaulagiri I and Tukuche Peak from the East-Northeast
① Dhaulagiri I, 8167m ② Dhaulagiri I Southeast Ridge
③ Dhaulagiri I Northeast Ridge ④ Dhaulagiri I East Face
⑤ Dhaulagiri I North Face ⑥ Tukuche Peak, 6920m
⑦ Dhaulagiri IV, 7661m ⑧ Dhaulagiri II, 7751m
⑨ Churen Himal, 7371m ⑩ French Pass, 5334m

The 1950 French group led by Maurice Herzog set up a base camp in Tukuche and conducted a very extensive reconnaissance of the northern and eastern slopes of Dhaulagiri I. French Pass was named in their honor.

44. Putha Hiunchuli and Churen Himal from the East-Southeast
① Putha Hiunchuli, 7246m ② Churen Himal, 7371m
③ Dhaulagiri VI, 7268m ④ Gurja Himal, 7193m

The terrain forming the mountains stretching from the Himalaya to the Tibetan Plateau, formerly an ocean bottom, is seen here sloping gently toward Tibet, to the north.

Putha Hiunchuli was easily climbed by Jimmy Roberts in 1954. Churen Himal was first climbed in 1970 by a Japanese team led by Takashi Serizawa. Gurja Himal was climbed in 1969 by a Japanese team led by Yoshimi Yakushi.

45. The village of Phortse clings to a tiny bit of flat land

Himalayan villages are welcome rest stops for both mountaineers and trekkers. Even when viewed during a flight, the green and geometrical shapes of the houses give welcome relief from the expanses of rock and snow.

As you climb the valleys that run north-south through the Himalaya, you find villages cleverly constructed on tiny plots of gently rolling land, clinging to the steep slopes of the valley walls. These are linked across steep passes by long winding trails. This is the Himalaya!

PHOTOGRAPHIC DATA

NO.	MO/DAY/YR	TIME	ALTITUDE	LENS	FILTER			
1.	5/3/83	0805	6700m	W125mm	1B			
2.	2/17/92	1530	7700m	W150mm	1B			
3.	5/3/83	0810	6700m	W125mm	1B	E		
4.	5/3/83	0800	6200m	W125mm	1B	EH		
5.	5/3/83	0815	6700m	W125mm	1B	EPD		
6.	5/3/83	0825	7000m	W125mm	1B	EPD		
7.	11/4/92	0940	8900m	W125mm	1B	EPD		
8.	11/4/92	0850	8800m	SW90mm	CF	EPD		
9.	4/24/79	0820	7200m	W150mm	SL	EPD③		
10.	11/4/92	0910	9000m	W150mm	1B	EPD		
11.	4/26/91	0620	8200m	W150mm	1B	RPD	f	
12.	4/6/92	0605	7200m	SW90mm	CF	EPD④	f1	
13.	9/26/91	0900	7400m	W150mm	1B+ND2	EPD	f13	1/500
14.	4/24/79	0810	6900m	SW105mm	SL	EPD③	*	*
15.	11/11/76	*	7500m	SW105mm	SL	EH①	*	*
16.	4/24/79	*	*	*	*	*	*	*
17.	9/27/91	0730	6800m	W150mm	1B	EPD	f11	1/500
18.	10/22/90	0700	7500m	W150mm	1B	EPD	f13	1/500
19.	4/10/92	0930	*	SW90mm	CF	EPD	f18	1/250
20.	4/27/91	0800	7200m	W125mm	1B	EPD	f18	1/500
21.	11/4/92	1150	5200m	W150mm	1B	EPD	f16	1/500
22.	9/24/91	0915	7300m	W125mm	1B+ND2	EPD①	f13	1/500
23.	5/4/83	0820	5700m	W125mm	1B	EPD	f16	1/500
24.	2/15/92	1740	6700m	W150mm	1B	EPD	f13	1/250
25.	9/24/91	0840	7300m	W125mm	1B+ND2	EPD①	f11	1/500
26.	4/7/92	0710	5800m	W125mm	1B	EPD	f16	1/500
27.	4/7/92	0740	5800m	W125mm	1B	EPD	f16	1/500
28.	9/27/91	1725	8000m	W150mm	1B	EPD	f11	1/500
29.	9/27/91	1725	8000m	W150mm	1B	EPD	f11	1/500
30.	9/27/91	1720	7900m	W125mm	1B	EPD	f11	1/500
31.	*	*	*	*	*	SL	*	*
32.	9/27/91	1730	8000m	W150mm	1B	EPD	f11	1/500
33.	11/5/76	*	*	W150mm	SL	EH	*	*
34.	11/5/76	*	8400m	W150mm	SL	EH①	*	*
35.	9/28/91	0650	7600m	W150mm	1B	EPD④	f11	1/500
36.	9/27/91	1710	8000m	W125mm	1B	EPD	f13	1/500
37.	11/5/76	*	8400m	SW105mm	SL	EH②	*	*
38.	11/6/92	0810	*	W125mm	1B	EPD	f16	1/500
39.	9/28/91	0750	8100m	W150mm	1B	EPD	f13	1/500
40.	9/28/91	0640	8000m	W125mm	1B	EPD	f16	1/500
41.	9/28/91	0650	7600m	W150mm	1B	EPD④	f16	1/500
42.	9/28/91	0720	7900m	W125mm	1B	EPD	f16	1/500
43.	9/28/91	0740	7800m	W125mm	1B	EPD	f11	1/500
44.	9/28/91	0730	7500m	W150mm	1B	EPD	f13	1/500
45.	9/27/91	0730	4000m	W125mm	1B	EPD	f11	1/250

* data not available

① pulled 1/3 ② pushed 1/3 ③ pushed 1/2 ④ pushed 2/3

ACKNOWLEDGMENTS

Publication of this book was made possible by the cooperation of many people.

First, I would like to thank Chris Bonington for writing a wonderful introduction. Next I thank Yugo Ono for verifying the names of mountains and for his chapter on the formation of the Himalaya. Takayuki Shiraiwa, Shunji Iwata and Teiji Watanabe also assisted in verifying mountain names.

My flights over the Himalaya would not have been possible without the assistance of Machiko Tajika, Ang Gyaltsen, Hanji Ohgawara and particularly Takashi Miyahara. I am deeply indebted to the pilots: Emil Wick, Bishar Duan and M. J. Shrestha. Aircraft maintenance was capably handled by Mr. Khal, B. K. Shrestha and Naofumi Takeshita. Cooperation was provided by the Himalayan Tourism Association

Tomoya Iozawa and Seiichi Hatano introduced me to the pleasures of reading topography.

In making my high-performance panorama camera I was ably assisted by Yohtaro Kobayashi, Yasuo Honda, Katsuhiro Ohtake, the late Kentaro Hattori, Junichi Hattori and Nobuji Iida. Tokiro Moriya and Jinichiro Maeda accompanied me on some flights, adding to the enjoyment of the trips.

The Japanese text was translated into English by Harold Solomon; this translation is also the basis for all of the European-language editions. Toshio Inoue was the book designer. The map was prepared by Senshusha.

Publication of this book was made possible by the cooperation of Yoshimitsu Kawasaki, Kazuya Kimura, Shigeo Endo, Tsunemichi Ikeda and Kyoko Tanaka. Printing was handled, under the direction of Etsuo Kamijo, by numerous helpful employees of Dai Nippon Printing Co. and Dai Nippon Total Process Ichigaya

Many others kindly offered their assistance and encouragement; I regret that it is not possible to mention each one individually.

ABOUT THE AUTHORS

Koichiro Ohmori

Born in Tokyo in 1935. Graduated from the Department of Applied Chemistry, School of Engineering, Keio University in 1957. Belonged to the Alpine Club while a student and climbed many mountains. Member of the Club's Himal Chuli expedition after graduation. Obtained a private pilot's license in 1972.

Employed for a time by Honshu Paper K.K.; presently Chief of the Water Environment Operations Division, Nippon Core K.K. Currently a Managing Director of the Japanese Alpine Club, with responsibility for nature conservation activities.

Designed and produced his own panorama cameras, and has had many panoramic photos published in books and magazines. Books include *Aerial Photographs of Northern Japanese Alps, Aerial Photographs of Japan's Famous Mountains* and *Aerial Panoramas of the Northern Japanese Alps* [all published by Yama-Kei Publishers] and *Fly Over Mountains* [Iwanami].

Yugo Ono

Born in Tokyo in 1948. Graduated from the Department of Geology and Mineralogy, Faculty of Science, Tokyo University of Education in 1970. Received his doctorate from the same University in 1975. Currently Professor in the Graduate School of Earth Environmental Science of Hokkaido University.

Member of the Japanese Alpine Club and Executive Committee member of the Association of Japanese Geographers, Japanese Association for Quaternary Research and Nature Conservation Society of Japan.

Published books include *Trip to the Ice Age as Seen by the Gods* (coauthored with Koichiro Ohmori) [Maruzen], *Natural History of Hokkaido* (coauthored with Yaeko Igarashi) [Hokkaido University Press] and translation of *The Periglacial Environment* (by H. M. French) [Kokon-shoin].